BECOMING

RICH

AND

WEALTHY

SECRETS TO
FINANCIAL PROSPERITY

JOE-JESIMIEL OGBE

Becoming Rich And Wealthy

All scripture quotations are from the King James Version of the Bible, except otherwise stated.

ISBN: 978-978-55429-29

Published in Nigeria by:

YOUNG DISCIPLES PRESS

Printed In Nigeria by:

Livingproof Press Limited

1, Heal The World Avenue, Opposite Shoprite, Sango Ota, Ogun State.

For further information or permission, contact:

DIRECTOR OF PUBLICATIONS,

Young Disciples International (Ydi)

3, YDI Street off Isheri-LASU Road (By Hotel Solous B/Stop), Igando, Lagos

Tel: 01-2934286, 08023124455

E-mail: joejesimiel2006@yahoo.com

www.ydiworld.org

CONTENTS

DEDICATION

Dr Tola and Wumi Olukilede

PREFACE

Have you seen a poor person becoming rich and wealthy? And have you ever seen a rich man becoming poor before? In the course of writing, one of my protégés in the UK called to tell me how a colleague of his who used to be wealthy became bankrupt and penniless. This guy is not finding life easy at all. It is better a poor man becomes rich, than for a rich man to become poor! My prayer is that through this book, your poverty shall be converted to prosperity! And if you have tasted a little bit of riches and wealth, God will cause you to become richer and wealthier in Jesus' name!

As God's servant, I prophetically decree and declare that your financial future shall be colorful, current economic downturn notwithstanding. Even if you are as poor as a church rat, your case is not as horrible as the devil wants you to believe. My God is still in the business of raising the poor out of the dust and lifting the needy out of the dunghills. I see Him raising you and making you rich and wealthy. I see Him causing you to eat the riches of the gentles. "But ye shall be named the Priests of the LORD: men shall call you the Ministers of our God: ye shall eat the riches of the Gentiles, and in their glory shall ye boast yourselves." (Isaiah 61:6)

You shall enjoy the wealth of nations and boast about the riches you receive from them! For there shall be a mega wealth transfer - from Gentiles to God's children very soon. And you shall be a major beneficiary and a partaker in Jesus' name.

This book in your hand is my candid attempt to debunk some erroneous beliefs or mindsets about wealth, and to set you on the pathway to sustainable economic empowerment and growth. I'm also using this book as a wake-up call to awaken your consciousness about wealth as enshrined in the Word of God.

The following ten biblical truths about wealth would serve as an appetizer for you even as I prepare to serve you the main course. Please I urge you to meditate and internalize them into your heart:

1. *The Lord gives His people the power to get wealth*

"But thou shalt remember the LORD thy God: for it is he that giveth thee power to get wealth, that he may establish his covenant which he sware unto thy fathers, as it is this day." Deuteronomy 8:18

"Wisdom and knowledge is granted unto thee; and I will give thee riches, and wealth, and honour, such as none of the kings have had that have been before thee, neither shall there any after thee have the like."

2 Chronicles 1:12

2. *Wealth and riches are in the house of the righteous*

"His seed shall be mighty upon earth: the generation of the upright shall be blessed.

Wealth and riches shall be in his house: and his righteousness endureth for ever."

Ps 112:2-3

3. *Wealth is a strong city*

"The rich man's wealth is his strong city: the destruction of the poor is their poverty."

Proverbs 10:15

4. *Wealth increases or decreases*

"Wealth gotten by vanity shall be diminished: but he that gathereth by labour shall increase."

Proverbs 13:11

5. *Wealth makes many friends*

"Wealth maketh many friends; but the poor is separated from his neighbour."

Proverbs 19:4

6. *Enjoying your wealth is the gift of God*

"Every man also to whom God hath given riches and wealth, and hath given him power to eat thereof, and to take his portion, and to rejoice in his labour; this is the gift of God."

Ecclesiastes 5:19

7. *Wealth of the sinner is laid up for the just*

"A good man leaveth an inheritance to his children's children: and the wealth of the sinner is laid up for the just."

Proverbs 13:22

8. *Some people trust in their wealth*

"They that trust in their wealth, and boast themselves in the multitude of their riches; 7 None of them can by any means redeem his brother, nor give to God a ransom for him:"

Ps 49:6-7

9. *Some people think their wealth is a function of their power*

"And thou say in thine heart, My power and the might of mine hand hath gotten me this wealth." Deuteronomy 8:17

10. *Beware of Evil disease of wealth*

"A man to whom God hath given riches, wealth, and honour, so that he wanteth

nothing for his soul of all that he desireth, yet God giveth him not power to eat thereof, but a stranger eateth it: this is vanity, and it is an evil disease."

Ecclesiastes 6:2

INTRODUCTION

The Bible says, "Moreover the profit of the earth is for all: the king himself is served by the field." (Ecclesiastes 5:9)

From the above scripture, it is crystal clear that all humans are meant to enjoy the

wealth or profit of the earth! But how come some people are enjoying the profit of the earth and others are not? Are the rich and wealthy people created wealthy and the poor people created poor? No! Not at all! God did not create some people wealthy and others poor. Just as people can become rich, people can become poor also. The Bible says, "He becometh poor that dealeth with a slack hand: but the hand of the diligent maketh

rich." (Proverbs 10:4)

The wealthy are rich because they know how to create wealth - they know and do certain things that command wealth, while on the other hand, the poor

7

are not fully acquainted with the "know-how" of wealth creation or they are simply lazy!

I have discovered that rich and wealthy people work smart, make the right and smart choices! They see opportunities and maximize them, while the poor do not. The poor are a bunch of lazy consumers, they spend their money on consumables. Wealthy People understand and practically engage in saving and investment. They are always seeking avenues to multiply their money by investing in assets. The rich know how to identify opportunities by taking well calculated risk. They don't rely on luck or handouts from benefactors, like the poor.

While poor people are relying on luck, the wealthy are working diligently, tenaciously and concertedly with a view to creating wealth.

"Becoming Rich and Wealthy" is the book for the hour! It is a timely reading material designed to impart wisdom for wealth creation. If you are tired of living a life of average and poverty or if your greatest ambition is to become rich and wealthy, then you are the reason for this book.

Wealth is not the exclusive preserve of a few! God has designed wealth and riches for all of us. All we need to do is, change our wealth-limiting mentality to wealth-creating mentality, so as to secure our financial prosperity with ease.

I'm of firm conviction that the first step to take in order to secure financial prosperity is to dislike or have a deep-seated aversion to poverty. You must passionately hate poverty, because the destruction of the poor is their poverty. If you don't want to be destroyed, then you must hate and dislodge poverty from your life. As a person, I began to develop a deep-seated aversion to poverty when I read from scriptures that a poor man's wisdom is always despised, and his voice is not heard in high places of the world, no matter how impactful and credible his contributions. The Biblical passage that transformed my mentality is Ecclesiastes 9:14-16: "There was a little city, and few men within it; and there came a great king against it, and besieged it, and built great bulwarks against it: Now there was found in it a poor wise man, and he by his wisdom delivered the city; yet no man remembered that same poor man. Then said I, Wisdom is better than strength: nevertheless the poor man's wisdom is despised, and his words are not heard."

As a people, we must rise up against poverty. As an individual, the earlier you declare a total war against poverty the better for you. For goodness sake, why must you be unperturbed in the midst of economic and social misery? Why must you be comfortable suffering from low productivity or earning low and meagre salaries? You find it difficult to pay basic bills, feed your family, pay your children's school fees or house rents, and you sit there saying, "It's the will of God!" Who told you God is responsible for your lack or poverty? Are you now saying God is out to destroy you? Have you not read that the destruction of the poor is their poverty? The Bible says, "The rich man's wealth is his strong city: the destruction of the poor is their poverty." (Proverbs 10:15)

God is not the reason why you are suffering. No! As a loving Father, God is much more concerned about your personal and family wellbeing. He is bringing you into a "wealthy place"! My Bible says, "... thou broughtest us out into a wealthy place." (Psalms 66:12)

As a servant of God, I decree and declare that God of all riches and wealth, will bring you to a wealthy place where poverty will no longer harass, molest and humiliate you; a place where you will no longer become vulnerable to sicknesses and diseases. I decree and declare that you will become rich and wealthy, so that you too will enjoy the good things of life! You shall spend your days in prosperity and your years in pleasures! The Bible says, "If they obey and serve him, they shall spend their days in prosperity, and their years in pleasures." (Job 36:11)

I'm of candid conviction that God inspired me to write this book primarily to show you how to escape poverty and position you for great riches and wealth.

As you immerse yourself in the following pages, keep this key point in your subconscious mind: that financial prosperity is possible, and that enduring or durable riches is also possible only on the account of the fact that you are willing to embrace God's timeless principles for wealth creation. It is very important that you know also that God wants you to be rich and wealthy so that you could use your wealth to advance His kingdom on earth! He is set to prosper you beyond measure so that you could contribute to the spreading of the gospel to nations of the world. The Bible says, "Cry yet, saying, Thus saith the LORD of hosts; My cities through prosperity shall yet be spread abroad; and the LORD shall yet comfort Zion, and shall yet choose Jerusalem." (Zechariah 1:17)

Tim Collins said in his book, Good to Great "that good is the enemy of great is not just a business problem. It is a human problem." Don't seek to become a good millionaire, but rather seek to become a great millionaire! Who is a great millionaire? A great millionaire is the rich person who uses his or her wealth to advance the worthy causes of God and humanity. He or she is not self centered or engaged in self-aggrandizement. May you become a great millionaire or billionaire in Jesus' name!

A wise man said, "The largest room on earth is the room for improvement!" Be prepared to keep improving your wealth creating strategies regularly if you don't want to be left behind. In this life, overtaking is permitted!

Today, we have many emerging millionaires and billionaires! They want to overtake the wealthy people of our generation. Who was Mark Zuckerberg, the founder of Facebook in the 1990s? But today, he's the third richest dude in town! God's desire for you is that your wealth will not diminish but grow from generation to generation. As the righteous of God, your financial path will be like the bright morning light, growing brighter and brighter until full day in Jesus' name! The Bible says, "But the path of the just is as the shining light, that shineth more and more unto the perfect day." (Proverbs 4:18)

No doubt, the profoundly articulated God's timeless secrets will engender your financial greatness and sustainable wealth, if only you are poised to embrace the instructions and advice in this life-changing book.

Happy Reading!

Joe Jesimiel Ogbe

October, 2017

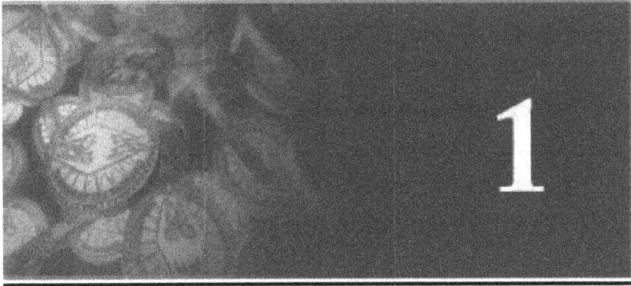

1 TAPPING INTO WEALTH CREATING POWER

One of Satan's greatest ploys or strategies is to get people to forget God's power as the true source of wealth. Satan has been in the business of making people believe that through diabolical power or human power, they can become rich and wealthy. Yes, they can, but their wealth will be laced with sorrow upon sorrow. The blessing or wealth from the Lord makes a person rich, and He adds no sorrow to it. The Bible says, "The blessing of the LORD, it maketh rich, and he addeth no sorrow with it."

(Proverbs 10:22)

God's power is the ultimate source of true wealth in the kingdom which we can readily tap into with ease. Moses told the children of Israel that: "And thou say in thine heart, My power and the might of mine hand hath gotten me this wealth. But thou shalt remember the LORD thy God: for it is he that giveth thee power to get wealth, that he may establish his covenant which he sware unto thy fathers, as it is this day."

(Deuteronomy 8:17-18)

One vital question is, will God be interested in giving us power to get wealth? Yes of course! God, as a wealthy Father is more than ready and prepared to make us wealthy! God can give us great wealth without reservation! Mega wealth comes from Him, not man or the devil. So don't make the mistake of tapping into wealth creating power seeking for wealth via other means, and miss out on God's blessings. And if you are depending on God's blessings to command riches and wealth, then let your eyes be focused on Him alone! I have heard of some so called Christians seeking God's power and devil's power at the same time.

3 ways to tap into Wealth Creating Power:

1. Become a bona fide child of God

Every father leaves an inheritance for his children! God, as a loving Father is not an exception! You and I can only tap into God's power by becoming His bona fide children. And as God's children, we are entitled to His resources - grace, power, blessings etc. Are you a child of God? Are you truly a bona fide son or daughter of God through Jesus Christ? The Bible says, "But as many as received him, to them gave he power to become the sons of God, even to them that believe on his name:" (John 1:12)

The place and importance of New birth with respect to the subject of riches and wealth cannot be over-emphasized, as salvation does not only deliver you from the shackles of sin and iniquity, but opens you to the financial treasure of God. The truth is that if God could give you His best, Jesus Christ, nothing else, wealth and riches inclusive, will be withheld from you! The Bible says, "He that spared not his own Son, but delivered him up for us all, how shall he not with him also freely give us all things?" (Romans 8:32)

2. *Place a demand for the Power*

God responds favorably to your requests or petition!

Jabez got a change of status by asking God for enlargement and blessings. The Bible says, "And Jabez called on the God of Israel, saying, Oh that thou wouldest bless me indeed, and enlarge my coast, and that thine hand might be with me, and that thou wouldest keep me from evil, that it may not grieve me! And God granted him that which he requested." (1 Chronicles 4:10)

No one becomes rich and wealthy in the kingdom of God without the grace or power of God! Prayer remains a vital key to accessing God's power and blessings. The Bible says, "Ask of me, and I shall give thee the heathen for thine inheritance, and the uttermost parts of the earth for thy possession." (Psalms 2:8)

To place a request or demand at the gates of heaven will require your humility. It takes humility to connect with more grace or power of God! The Bible says, "But he giveth more grace. Wherefore he saith, God resisteth the proud, but giveth grace unto the humble." (James 4:16)

God will exalt the humble but demote the proud.

You cannot tap into wealth creating power if there is pride in your life. Are you a proud person? Are you full of yourself? Always remember this: whatever wealth you command today or in the nearest future comes from God, as such, do not allow pride to raise its ugly head in your heart. If you begin to excel in business, if your bank accounts begin to explode via lodgments, never make the mistake of attributing it to your power, ability or expertise. Rather, attribute it to the grace and power of God at work in you. And as you do this heartily, you will keep soaring higher and higher.

It's not apt to bombard the Gates of heaven with prayer requests for more financial

blessings, when you have not really appreciated God with heartfelt thanksgiving for how He has blessed you thus far. Sustainable wealth is for those that will acknowledge God's inputs with heartfelt appreciation and thanksgiving. Thanking God will cause Him to exempt you and your business from the floods of life. Celebrating and appreciating God will make you to be delivered from the ups and downs of business. God will give you wisdom to escape the tsunami or holocaust in the business world. The grace and power of God can distinguish you from those that are chasing shadows or winds.

3. Stir Up the Power Within

According to Dr Myles Monroe, "Hidden within you, you have one of the most powerful tools unknown to mankind. One that has the capabilities to change the course of history. What is that tool? It is your God-given gift! "

You are gifted by God! And this gift is not something you learn or earn! It is something God has graciously given you. A gift is like a precious stone to the one who has it, and whenever he stirs it up, it turns into prosperity. "A gift is as a precious stone in the eyes of him that hath it: whithersoever it turneth, it prospereth" (Proverbs 17:8)

As a child of God, the power to create wealth is within you right now! At creation, God gave you a super creating "machine" called the brain! Your brain is a wonderful gift! And at new birth, He gave you the Holy Ghost power to command outstanding results in whatever area of human endeavors. But how come these powers are not yielding the required results? Because they have not been stirred up! What does it mean to stir? It means to mix or cause movement in a thing that has being in a state of dormancy. Many of us are carriers of these powers but without any form of activation! What a shame!

The Bible says, "Wherefore I put thee in remembrance that thou stir up the gift of God, which is in thee by the putting on of my hands. For God hath not given us the spirit of fear; but of power, and of love, and of a sound mind." (2 Tim 1:6-7) The word "stir" simply means to activate, to cause to become active and to bring into use. God has graciously given us the spirit of power, of love and sound mind! The gift – power of God, can be likened to a deposit of great treasure on your inside waiting to be stirred up. It is your non-transferable responsibility to stir up the power, no one can do this on your behalf. The level to which you enjoy the power deposit in you is determined by how much you activate it. You can stir up the gift within via prayers and spiritual engagement!

Orison S Marden said, "Deep within man dwell those slumbering powers; powers that would astonish him, that he never dreamed of possessing; forces that would revolutionize his life if aroused and put into action." You arouse this power by taking action!

Different actions produce different results. It's not what you do once a while that shapes or stirs up the power but what you do consistently.

Take a decision to do something consistently. You can't stir up the power for wealth creation by being interested in wealth creation, but it's by being committed to it. The power is stirred when you make a committed decision. Most rich people have this indomitable decision to make more money, hence the activation of the power.

Decision was the source of Queen Esther's power, as she prepared to meet the king. "If I perish, I perish" was her resolute decision to meet the king. If the poor person can take a decision to change his economic status, power within will rise up like a lion to deliver into his hands, great riches and wealth.

Anthony Robbins said, "True decisions are the catalyst for awakening the giant and dormant power within you!"

A wise man also said, "Concerning all acts of initiative and creation, there is one elementary truth – that the moment one definitely commits oneself, then providence moves, too." The moment Daniel purposed not to defile himself, grace and power was supplied to help him achieve his heart's desire. The Bible says, "But Daniel purposed in his heart that he would not defile himself with the portion of the king's meat, nor with the wine which he drank: therefore he requested of the prince of the eunuchs that he might not defile himself. Now God had brought Daniel into favour and tender love with the prince of the eunuchs."

(Daniel 1:8 – 9)

Do you really know how to make a decision?

I think the bane of poor people is that most of them don't recognize what it means to make a real decision. They don't know or realize the force or power of change that a committed decision creates.

Making a true decision means committing yourself to achieving a result. Information carries weight when it is acted upon! And there is no action without a decision!

My sincere prayer is that this book will motivate you to act upon every bit of information, advice and instruction therein. Make a decision that the power for wealth creation in you will not be lying dormant! Make a decision to engage your brain productively by reading, studying and researching. Someone said, "It is not enough to have a good mind, the main thing is to use it well." Your mind is such a magnificent gift you were born with. Your brain's capacity is nearly unfathomable. Not many of us know how it works to help us achieve what we want.

According to brain experts, "your brain eagerly awaits your every command, ready to carry out anything you ask of it." While rich people command their brains to yield wealth creation ideas and strategies via robust thinking or cogitation, poor people would rather allow dormancy to be their lot. If poor people can tell their brain that poverty is unbearable and that they want wealth and riches, the brain would release power to create riches and wealth for them!

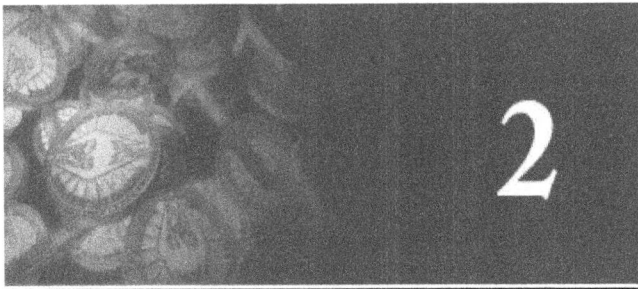

2 CONCEIVING IDEAS FOR WEALTH CREATION

"Ideas rule the world" is a popular cliché!

And this is because creations around us are products of ideas. This book you are reading right now, is my God-given idea to combat poverty. I got this idea while on missionary assignment to East African countries of Uganda, Rwanda, Kenya and Tanzania.

As humans, ideas or thoughts whether good or bad flow through us constantly. Some ideas could provoke actions, while others just evaporate into thin air. Have you had an idea to do something before? Have you conceived an idea and imagine its fulfillment? Whatever you will ever become or do in life is a function of an idea. To become rich and wealthy you need to conceptualize wealth creating ideas.

What is an idea?

An idea is a thought or suggestion as to a possible course of action. It is described as a plan formed by thinking. An idea therefore is about the application of the mental domain within the sphere of thought in order to arrive at a specific objective that is perceived as desirable, workable and favourable. A good idea is a good thought, which if developed and executed or applied properly, produces good and great beneficial results.

How to conceive ideas for wealth creation:

Focus your mind on the Word of God

You can conceive ideas for wealth creation by ordering or focusing your mind on the word of God and His promises that engender wealth and riches.

There are many passages in the Bible that talk about how God prospered His people. As you read the scriptures, ask God to give you pictures of your future. It's awesome to have a blueprint of where you are heading in life! God who gave Noah an idea to build an ark will do same for you! God who gave Jacob an idea to become a guru in agriculture- animal husbandry will do same for you! An idea to build a mega business or conglomerate shall be imparted to you as you read this book in Jesus' name!

Ask God for ideas

God remains the eternal Source or reservoir of ideas that will benefit man! God can help you access ideas through the power of illumination and revelation. Many people in the church have given testimonies of how they received business ideas from God via vision or dreams. If you pray for wealth creating ideas fervently and wholeheartedly, the Holy Spirit will place some thoughts, ideas or "graphic pictures" in your mind. Ideas can come in form of visions and dreams! Will the One who promised to prosper you not give you ideas of prosperity. Will the One who gave Israel power to get wealth, not give you divine ideas for wealth creation? Will the One who gave Jacob idea to multiply his wealth, not give you ideas? With God, you shall not be bereft or bankrupt of wealth creation ideas.

God's ideas are innumerable! Can you count the number of products which His ideas have produced?

God's idea produced man! And man's ideas have also produced so many things in our world! All the great and good ideas come from or originates from God. As children of God, we literally wallow in the sea of great divine ideas! We are at a great advantage because we can be spiritually quickened to communicate with God directly and receive fresh ideas from Him even on a daily basis. There are mighty ideas in the heart of God that could provoke a great revolution in wealth creation. All you have to do is to call on Him and He will show them to you! Beloved, there are many things or ideas which humanity is yet to uncover or unravel! The Bible says, "Call on me in prayer and I will answer you. I will show you great and mysterious things which you still do not know about." (Jeremiah 33:3 NET)

As you call on God, you will always get a continuous flow of ideas from Him.

Move with rich people

It is important that you know and understand that you can get ideas from people, especially wealthy people. Based on their experience, exposure, situation and world view, as you interact with them, you will be poised to conceive one idea or the other. Naturally, a typical rich person may not want to share his ideas, but you can get ideas as you discuss and chat with them. You need to be hyper sensitive! Decide to study them and learn from them. Read their stories and see what they went through. The secrets of men are in their stories! Their stories can inspire you with ideas. You can't become rich and wealthy by hanging around poor people! conceiving ideas for wealth creation

Don't move with anyone who will not spur you into creating wealth! You need to know what rich and wealthy people are doing to create wealth and follow their example.

Read Books and magazines

If you want to be rich and wealthy, you must be prepared to bury yourself in books and magazines.

Most of my rich and wealthy friends are avid readers. They read books that inspire or motivate them. They don't read for reading sake! They read to connect and rob minds with authors. Believe me, many books and magazines are loaded with ideas!

I do believe that the reason for poverty in Africa is that many of us do not have the culture of reading and researching like people in the developed world. On my way back from USA via Paris, I saw some of my black Africans sleeping or chatting all through the flight to Lagos, while some white folks were busy reading books or perusing magazines!

Bill Gates, the richest man on earth, stumbled on an idea for portable computers from a magazine!

Go for books! Make books and magazines your good friends! It will also be apt to take advantage of the Internet. Some people, even young folks have accessed wealth creating ideas from the Internet. When you visit or browse the net, which site do you normally go to? I urge you to visit business ideas, innovation or promotion sites.

Observe things in your Environment

There are so many wealth creating ideas in your environment! As you move around your communities or towns, cities and countries, open your physical and inner eyes! Don't be surprised as you might be inspired with wealth creating ideas! Someone went to India and saw real poverty, as people there were not wearing shoes. Another person went to the same India and saw great opportunity to make shoes for the teeming population of people not wearing shoes. As you observe or look intently around you, ask God to help you see beyond the surface! Wealth creating ideas and opportunities are not open to all eyes!

Warning

Satan has the capacity to use people, places, events, creatures, or even circumstances to inject his evil ideas into any man and woman. Every destructive idea is from the devil! Don't present him the opportunity! The Bible says, "Then entered Satan into Judas surnamed Iscariot, being of the number of the twelve. And he went his way, and communed with the chief priests and captains, how he might betray him unto them." (Luke 22:3-4)

If Satan could inject into Judas the idea of betraying or selling his Master, then you must be watchful and vigilant, so that the devil will not take a foothold in your mind.

Any wealth creating idea that does not glorify God and promote His agenda must be jettisoned. For instance, God cannot be in support of an idea to run a brothel or club. In the course of writing, Nigerian media, both traditional news and social media, have been awash with the news of how a young man in his thirties made billions of Naira through kidnapping and hostage taking business. Any idea of making money through criminality or diabolical means is not from God!

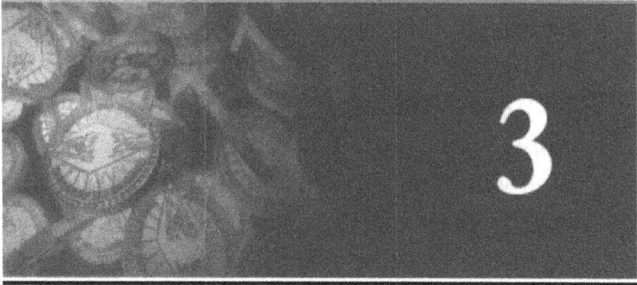

3 CULTIVATING THE ATTITUDE OF THE WEALTHY

The truth is that wealthy people think differently from poor people. Rich people have a wealth creating mindset! Attitude is a predisposition, a settled way of thinking or a tendency that provokes a certain behavior or action. Wealthy people have a settled way of thinking that engenders wealth creation. I have billionaire friends, and I can tell you that they are always thinking of how to create or make more money!

Someone said, "There's no shortage of money on planet Earth, only a shortage of people who think correctly about it." To become rich and wealthy, you must put a stop to your poverty thinking. Put an end to your wealth-limiting mentality! No one becomes wealthy without thinking or cultivating the attitude of the wealthy. If you want to be a millionaire, think like a millionaire! And if you want to be a billionaire, think like a billionaire! It's possible you're poor simply because you have allowed or beclouded your mind with poverty inducing thoughts. You can't be thinking poor and expect to be rich! You are the product of your thoughts! The Bible says, "For as he thinketh in his heart, so is he..." (Proverbs 23:7)

From scriptures, and even from our contemporary world, we have many veritable examples of people who have attained what we want to attain and there is no doubt about this, except we want to deceive ourselves or engage in arrogance. There are people whose wealth creation skills have energized them to command outstanding wealth in life. Just Google and you will find Christians who are blazing the trail as far as wealth creation is concerned. We are enjoined to learn from them and follow their example! The Bible says, "That ye be not slothful, but followers of them who through faith and patience inherit the promises." (Hebrews 6:12)

Father Abraham

Father Abraham remains our indefatigable father of faith. He is our pattern of faith in the Bible. He is also our patterned template of a super rich and wealthy man in his generation. He exemplified and epitomized biblical wealth! Abraham was greatly blessed with great riches. No wonder, we are enjoined to look up to him. "Look unto Abraham your father, and unto Sarah that bare you: for I called him alone, and blessed him, and increased him." (Isaiah 51:2)

Abraham was greatly blessed and greatly enriched by God, that his servant even gave a testimony thus: "The Lord has richly blessed my master and he has become very wealthy. The Lord has given him sheep and cattle, silver and gold, male and female servants, and camels and donkeys." (Genesis 24:35 NET)

What was Abraham's attitude? What was his mindset or settled way of thinking? His attitude was that of absolute dependence on God for prosperity. He had the mentality of creating his own wealth via divine providence. Abraham never wanted any man to lay claim to his wealth. "That I will not take from a thread even to a shoelatchet, and that I will not take any thing that is thine, lest thou shouldest say, I have made Abram rich:" (Genesis 14:23)

Abraham was never waiting on any man for help. He looked up to God as the major help for his wealth creation. Poor people have the propensity toward looking up to government, donor agencies and friends to help them out. Poor people think or believe the road to wealth is through the help of others. I'm reliably informed that some poor African nations wait for foreign aids before passing their national budget! What a shame! What an absurdity! They are incapacitated and rendered impotent if help does not come from donor countries and agencies. If you want to be wealthy like Abraham, then don't wait on any man. Just develop the attitude of absolute dependence on God for your wealth. Trust God to impart you with divine ideas and wisdom to create wealth. Trust in His power and grace only, for no man can make you wealthy without the support or approval of God! The Bible says, "... A man can receive nothing, except it be given him from heaven." (John 3:27)

So don't allow any man lay claim or brag that he made you rich. Let no man share the glory that is due to God!

Understand that Abraham was a super prosperous man, and at same time a friend of God. "And the scripture was fulfilled which saith, Abraham believed God, and it was imputed unto him for righteousness: and he was called the Friend of God." (James 2:23)

Father God in the light of your word, that says, "And if ye be Christ's, then are ye Abraham's seed, and heirs according to the promise." I hereby use my faith in Jesus Christ. I take delivery of my wealth which you packaged in Abraham and his seed.

I hereby decree and declare that the Abrahamic blessing be released upon me right now.

My hour of prosperity is here at last.

Poverty shall no longer molest or harass me!

Lord, as you enrich me with great wealth, I shall be a blessing to my generation in Jesus' name!

Isaac

Isaac is another biblical template of a wealthy person! The Bible says, "The man became wealthy. His influence continued to grow until he became very prominent." (Genesis 26:13 NET)

Isaac was a determined person. Determination is an attribute of the rich and wealthy. Being determined is about a resolute commitment to a given course. Isaac was not perturbed by the antics of the opposition. He determined to succeed in his business. Remember that on so many occasions, the Philistines had frustrated his efforts but he never gave up. He was never discouraged, he kept at it until he succeeded. "And he removed from thence, and digged another well; and for that they strove not: and he called the name of it Rehoboth; and he said, For now the LORD hath made room for us, and we shall be fruitful in the land." (Genesis 26:22)

Do you want to be rich and wealthy like Isaac? Then try to cultivate the attitude of determination, resolve to follow your passion cum assignment without allowing distraction or detractors. Most rich people even in our contemporary world, are men and women who usually will never give up on their objective or passion.

Develop the attitude of diligence. Isaac was a diligent man, who worked so hard to command great wealth. He was not a lazy man at all. Riches or wealth is not a product of luck or wishes! There is no wealth for the idle or indolent! Isaac was a worker!

Isaac also had the "I can-do" attitude which promoted his work ethics. He looked at situations in a positive light, thereby developing a sense of motivation and enthusiasm. Isaac was highly effective due to the attitude of meditation! "And Isaac went out to meditate in the field at the eventide... " (Genesis 24:63)

One of my billionaire friends loves to pray and meditate in the early hours of the morning! Daily practices of prayer and meditation can help keep you grounded, granting you the energy to have a "can-do" attitude. You can't connect with divinity and be ordinary! If you want to become rich and wealthy, cultivate the "I can-do attitude" via your faith in Christ Jesus! The Bible says, "I can do all things through Christ which strengtheneth me." (Philippians 4:13)

Isaac's disposition and reaction go to show us one rare quality of rich people. He never allowed a single failure to stop or destroy him. Each time he failed, he would bounce back as if nothing happened. I presume he kind of reminded himself of divine support and decided to forge ahead in the given task. Do you easily give up or get fed up? Change your attitude now!

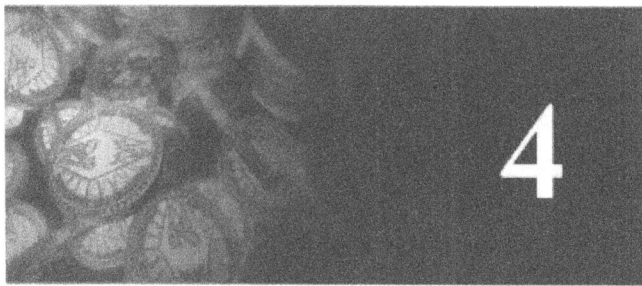

4 EMBRACING THE
DILIGENCE OF THE RICH

One of the very outstanding secrets to becoming super rich and wealthy is diligence! Rich people are known for diligence! They don't eat the bread of idleness like average or poor people, as they have mastered the art of diligence! They know how to be persistent and hard-working in their assignment or business. They are consumed by their hunger and hunt for wealth, so much so that they work assiduously to the point that they feel they are winning and not just working.

Wealth doesn't answer to just your ideas or mentality, wealth answers to diligence! The Bible says, "He becometh poor that dealeth with a slack hand: but the hand of the diligent maketh rich." (Proverbs 10:4)

What is Diligence?

Diligence refers to being persistent and making hard work effort in doing something. According to Webster's dictionary, diligence is about steady application in business; constant in effort or exertion to accomplish what is undertaken. It is about giving attention to your assignment without being careless or negligent.

Diligent people see what needs to be done; and they do it, and do it, and do it until they get the desired result. Isaac is my biblical business man who typified diligence. Isaac didn't stop because he got tired of digging the well! He didn't stop because Philistines opposed him! He didn't stop because the effect of famine was excruciating! He didn't stop because his business was taking a long time to get results! Nothing stopped Isaac from achieving results, nothing shall stop you too!

Diligence is indicative of a process. Rich people follow the due process of their business. They know that wealth and riches come by hard-work and poverty comes by indolence. "How long wilt thou sleep, O sluggard? when wilt thou arise out of thy sleep? Yet a little sleep, a little slumber, a little folding of the hands to sleep: So shall thy poverty come as one that travelleth, and thy want as an armed man." (Proverbs 6:9-11)

Have a Business

"Seest thou a man diligent in his business? he shall stand before kings; he shall not stand before mean men." (Proverbs 22:29) Before diligence there must be a business in place! You can't be diligent doing nothing. Before you can be diligent, you must diligently learn what you are supposed to be doing in life. There are many businesses out there which could make you rich and wealthy. You could be a career or professional person, farmer, technocrat, an entertainer or entrepreneur and what have you! Once you know your business or assignment, you can now commit yourself to it with all diligence.

Diligence is a virtue

Our Lord Jesus is our perfect example of someone who embraced the virtue of diligence. He was consistently and persistently committed to His Father's business while on earth. "And he said unto them, How is it that ye sought me? wist ye not that I must be about my Father's business?" (Luke 2:49)

Diligence is a Christ like attribute or virtue that must be embraced and cultivated by all of us. You and I can be as diligent as Christ was, and is.

As you show persistent and hardworking effort in doing your business, very soon you will become rich and wealthy.

Diligence is needed in all spheres of life as it is one of the key ingredients for success. Those who use the sheer power of diligence, succeed in their assignments. If you are a business man, you can make yourself successful in your business on the basis of your diligence. Becoming rich and wealthy will require 99.9 % commitment and in order to stay committed you must be diligent. Poverty is the portion of indolent folks! Kindly remind yourself of the drawbacks or downsides of sitting idle and doing nothing! Do you want to suffer hunger? The Bible says, "Slothfulness casteth into a deep sleep; and an idle soul shall suffer hunger." (Proverbs 19:15)

God does not bless nothing or empty hands! He blesses the work of your hands. God cannot bless laziness, idleness, lethargy and procrastination! An idle person is known as good-for-nothing. There is no real pleasure in sitting idle or slumbering! Wake up!

You need to be active to keep working toward becoming rich and wealthy.

May I end this chapter by emphasizing Solomon's words in Ecclesiastes 9:10: "Whatever your hand finds to do, do it with your might" - that is, whatever you do, do it to the best of your strength, ability or capacity. I pray that God may bless you with great riches and wealth, even as you embrace the secret of diligence!

The Bible says, "When Isaac planted in that land, he reaped in the same year a hundred times what he had sown, because the Lord blessed him. The man became wealthy. His influence continued to grow until he became very prominent. He had so many sheep and cattle and such a great household of servants that the Philistines became jealous of him." (Genesis 26:12-14 NET)

Be like Isaac! It takes diligence to plant! Hundred fold result is the reward of diligence! One solid truth you need to know about Isaac is that God did not just bless him because he was a covenant son, God blessed him because of his diligence! A diligent believer will command riches and wealth! An indolent believer will wallow in extreme poverty and penury! The choice is yours!

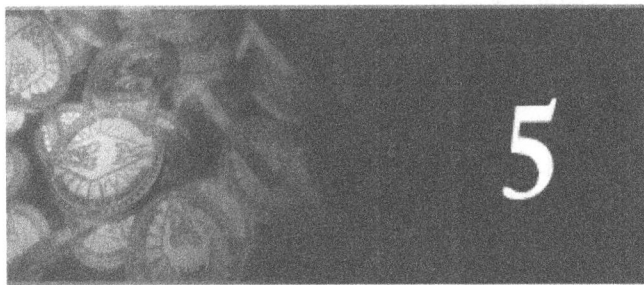

5 EMBRACING THE COVENANT DIMENSION OF WEALTH

The covenant keeping God has the capacity to pick you out of poverty and throw you into the realm of super wealth and riches, if only you can become a covenant practitioner. Practicing the covenant is about accepting and doing what the word of God says concerning prosperity. In the kingdom of God, people are poor not because the economy is poor! They are poor because they lack the knowledge of prosperity, they lack the knowledge and understanding of what the Word says, or even of what Jesus did for them. How many believers truly know that Jesus became poor so that through His poverty we might become rich? Grace of Salvation or redemption provokes great riches! The Bible says, "For ye know the grace of our

Lord Jesus Christ, that, though he was rich, yet for your sakes he became poor, that ye through his poverty might be rich." (2Cor. 8:9)

Bishop David Oyedepo said, "Prosperity in the kingdom does not answer to fasting and prayer!

Prosperity is not a promise you claim in prayers!

It only answers to your understanding and practice of covenant details or requirements."

Your quest to becoming super rich and wealthy will become a reality on the platform of the covenant practice. God is a covenant keeper. His side of every covenant is forever settled. It is on our side that we have issues. God is only committed when you apply yourself to the demands. You must enter into the covenant deliberately. "And they entered into a covenant to seek the LORD God of their fathers with all their heart and with all their soul" (2Chro. 15: 12)

You don't pray or fast for a covenant, you enter into it. You sign in for it. Why must you sign in?

Because the power to get wealth is released on the platform of the covenant of prosperity.

God's covenant is as eternal as day and night. Until you can stop day and night, you can't stop the covenant from yielding results. "Thus saith the LORD; If my covenant be not with day and night, and if I have not appointed the ordinances of heaven and earth; Then will I cast away the seed of Jacob, and David my servant, so that I will not take any of his seed to be rulers over the seed of Abraham, Isaac, and Jacob: for I will cause their captivity to return, and have mercy on them." (Jeremiah 33:25-26)

Covenant Responsibilities

1. Plant your Seed

The Bible says, "While the earth remaineth, seedtime and harvest, and cold and heat, and summer and winter, and day and night shall not cease." (Gen 8:22)

God's covenant works for every generation of believers. It is working in our generation right now!

As a young boy following my dad to the farm, we never lifted up our hands to pray without working. Yam won't come out of the ground until yam has gone into the earth! Harvest only answers to what you sow. There is no adverse economic crisis that is strong or powerful enough to break the efficacy of the covenant. Famine is not your problem!

Famine or no famine Isaac sowed his seed!

"Then Isaac sowed in that land, and received in the same year an hundredfold: and the LORD blessed him. And the man waxed great, and went forward, and grew until he became very great: For he had possession of flocks, and possession of herds, and great store of servants: and the Philistines envied him." (Genesis 26: 12-14)

If famine could not stop Isaac, famine cannot stop you also. The economy of Nigeria should not determine your prosperity. With all the economic downturns there are people smiling to their banks in Nigeria. There are people receiving fat credit alerts! Not everyone is suffering! That's the candid truth! Today, some people are offering their homes or treasures for sale; some other persons are prevailing and buying those stuffs cheaply!

Many Africans escaping the hardships at home have drowned in the high sea. Others have sold themselves as slaves to white people. That is the tragedy of Africa. But covenant practice can separate you from others. You shall not suffer like others! No nation is exempt from famine! So don't run to America or Europe. Covenant practice will exempt you from famine! Without a covenant covering, you remain a victim wherever you go.

2. Live righteously

In the kingdom of God, it's only the righteous that can flourish in super wealth and riches! The Bible says, "The righteous shall flourish like the palm tree: he shall grow like a cedar in Lebanon. Those that be planted in the house of the LORD shall flourish in the courts of our God. They shall still bring forth fruit in old age; they shall be fat and flourishing;" (Ps 92:12-14)

Embrace righteousness as a lifestyle! Don't cut corners. Don't engage in sharp practices in a bid to become rich and wealthy. You will not go far on the high way of corruption. Change your evil ways! Put away every form of iniquity and you will have plenty of silver! The Bible says, "If thou return to the Almighty, thou shalt be built up, thou shalt put away iniquity far from thy tabernacles. Then shalt thou lay up gold as dust, and the gold of Ophir as the stones of the brooks. Yea, the Almighty shall be thy defence, and thou shalt have plenty of silver." (Job 22:23-25)

3. Give God your tithe and offerings

These days, many people in church who are desiring God's blessing of wealth and riches, are busy robbing God in tithes and offerings. The Bible says, "Even from the days of your fathers ye are gone away from mine ordinances, and have not kept them. Return unto me, and I will return unto you, saith the LORD of hosts. But ye said, Wherein shall we return? Will a man rob God? Yet ye have robbed me. But ye say, Wherein have we robbed thee? In tithes and offerings. Ye are cursed with a curse: for ye have robbed me, even this whole nation. Bring ye all the tithes into the storehouse, that there may be meat in mine house, and prove me now herewith, saith the LORD of hosts, if I will not open you the windows of heaven, and pour you out a blessing, that there shall not be room enough to receive it. And I will rebuke the devourer for your sakes, and he shall not destroy the fruits of your ground; neither shall your vine cast her fruit before the time in the field, saith the LORD of hosts. And all nations shall call you blessed: for ye shall be a delightsome land, saith the LORD of hosts." Mal 3:7-12

Your yieldedness to God in the aspect of tithing and giving of offering is what determines your prosperity. Until your heart is made up in obeying God in this vital covenant practice, your prosperity is not guaranteed. The tithe, which is the tenth part of your income is not yours. It belongs to God. Don't touch it. Give it honorably and joyfully.

4. Delight in God

The Bible says, "Delight thyself also in the LORD; and he shall give thee the desires of thine heart. Commit thy way unto the LORD; trust also in him; and he shall bring it to pass." (Ps 37:4-5)

It is the degree of your delight or affection for God that determines the fulfillment of your desires.

Do you desire to be rich and wealthy?

Then develop a heart for God! Do you want wealth and riches to be added to you? Then seek first God's kingdom and righteousness! "But seek ye first the kingdom of God, and his righteousness; and all these things shall be added unto you." (Mat 6:33)

5. Become a Giver

Until you accept the covenant terms of giving, you may not command wealth and riches as you should. God cannot entrust you with wealth, if He sees any trace of stinginess in you. Your wealth and riches will be determined by what you give! If you are a miser don't expect to prosper in the kingdom. Become a giver, even as we have been instructed by Lord to give! "Give, and it shall be given unto you; good measure, pressed down, and shaken together, and running over, shall men give into your bosom. For with the same measure that ye mete withal it shall be measured to you again." (Luke 6:38)

5 Kinds of Giving

1. Give to promote God's Kingdom

"O Lord our God, all this wealth, which we have collected to build a temple for you to honor your holy name, comes from you; it all belongs to you. I know, my God, that you examine thoughts and are pleased with integrity. With pure motives I contribute all this; and now I look with joy as your people who have gathered here contribute to you." (1 Chronicles 29:16-17 NET)

God gives you wealth so that you can give towards the promotion of His kingdom. Don't complain or murmur when a kingdom promotion demand is made in your church! Get excited each time you have an opportunity to give!

2. Give to your Pastor and other God's Prophets

"Now the one who receives instruction in the word must share all good things with the one who teaches it." (Galatians 6:6)

You are expected to give God's servants material and financial blessings which you have graciously received from God. As your pastor ministers spiritual food to you, it behooves you to sow or minister carnal things to him. Apostle Paul said, "It hath pleased them verily; and their debtors they are. For if the Gentiles have been made partakers of their spiritual things, their duty is also to minister unto them in carnal things." (Romans 15:27)

You are indebted to your pastor and other servants of God! As you share in their spiritual things, you are obligated also to minister to them in material things.

Don't forget, you will attract prophetic rewards as you consciously and deliberately provide for your pastor and other God's prophets. The Bible says, "He that receiveth a prophet in the name of a prophet shall receive a prophet's reward; and he that receiveth a righteous man in the name of a righteous man shall receive a righteous man's reward."(Matthew 10:41)

3. Give to the poor and needy

"He that hath pity upon the poor lendeth unto the LORD; and that which he hath given will he pay him again." (Proverbs 19:17)

You can't give to the poor, and be poor. When you give to poor and needy people you exempt yourself from poverty and lack. Poor people around you are divine opportunities for your financial prosperity. Reach out to them today and always. "One person is generous and yet grows more wealthy, but another withholds more than he should and comes to poverty. A generous person will be enriched, and the one who provides water for others will himself be satisfied." (Proverbs 11:24-25 NET)

4. Give to your parents

"Bring me venison, and make me savoury meat, that I may eat, and bless thee before the LORD before my death." (Genesis 27:7)

A venison in our context is anything or any amount of money given to your parents that provokes a blessing from them! God has loaded your parents, (both biological and spiritual) with power to bless and curse! It is wise to provoke their blessings via your giving instead of curses. These days, many children who are wealthy have forgotten their parents. What a shame! You attract curses instead of blessings if you abandon your parents!

5. Give towards worthy causes in the society

I like to affirm that one veritable purpose for your financial empowerment is for you to become relevant to humanity. It is for you to give towards worthy causes in the society. You can engage in Social action by attending to the needs of the hungry, destitute, sick, hopeless and homeless people. Job was involved in social action as a rich man. He said, "I was eyes to the blind, and feet was I to the lame. I was a father to the poor: and the cause which I knew not I searched out." (Job 29:15-16)

The goal or objective of social action is not to bring an Eldorado or utopian society to earth. Rather the goal is to make the situation a little better, a bit more tolerable and humane, more responsive to human needs, a better place for children to grow up, and perhaps provide a tiny glimpse of the Kingdom of God as modeled in your life. One way to demonstrate your love for God is by attending to the needs of people around you. Take a look around you, and you will see social needs begging for attention. As a Christian, you should be at the forefront of meeting the needs of the society. Prayerfully engage in a social action!

Two Outstanding Conditions for Giving

1. Give Willingly

Whatever you don't do willingly will not profit you. The Bible says, "The Israelites brought a freewill offering to the Lord, every man and woman whose heart was willing to bring materials for all the work that the Lord through Moses had commanded them to do." (Ex 35:29 NET)

David said, "But who am I, and what is my people, that we should be able to offer so willingly after this sort? for all things come of thee, and of thine own have we given thee." (1 Chronicles 29:14)

2. Give cheerfully or happily

The Bible says, "Every man according as he purposeth in his heart, so let him give; not grudgingly, or of necessity: for God loveth a cheerful giver." (2 Corinthians 9:7) God loves a cheerful giver! If He loves a cheerful giver, then He is most likely going to dislike anyone who gives grudgingly! A willing hearted giver, will be a cheerful giver.

Bishop David Oyedepo said, "Anything you present to God as if it's a burden, multiplies your burden."

It is a serious misdemeanor to serve God or give to Him without joyfulness and gladness of heart! You may even attract curses instead of blessings! The Bible says, "Because thou servedst not the LORD thy God with joyfulness, and with gladness of heart, for the abundance of all things; Therefore shalt thou serve thine enemies which the LORD shall send against thee, in hunger, and in thirst, and in nakedness, and in want of all things: and he shall put a yoke of iron upon thy neck, until he have destroyed thee." (Deuteronomy 28:47-48)

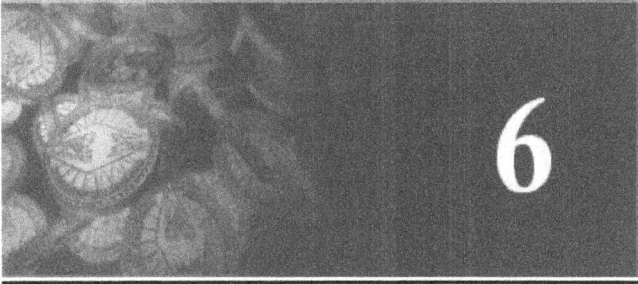

6 CULTIVATING INVESTMENT CULTURE

It has been said that the rich get richer and the poor get poorer. While we can fault the logic behind this saying (I'm sure we all know individuals who were once rich and now have nothing; or those who started out with nothing but are now wealthy), I must say there is a lot of truth in this saying.

You see, if there is no seed, there is no harvest; money is a seed and like any other seed, it will only grow if it is planted in fertile ground and nurtured. As such, the rich get richer because they have the necessary seed (money) needed to reap the harvest of wealth. Since we have surmised that money is a seed, we should all borrow a leaf from the farmer. A farmer never eats all that he harvests; rather he always saves a portion of his harvest to ensure that he has seed for the next planting season. In the same vein, if you want to become rich and wealthy, you must not eat your seed. Never spend all you earn because the wealth you desire to have in future, will only be harvested from the seeds of money you save or invest today. You may think you do not earn enough to save but do not be deceived. Start saving from what you have; start small and watch your little drops of savings become a pool of wealth!

While rich and wealthy people make it as a matter of lifestyle or culture to always save and invest; poor people on the other hand don't have this culture, they don't even care about saving or investing for the future, as they give the excuse that they don't have enough to spare or save.

What is Saving?

Saving is an income which you choose or decide deliberately not to spend, it also refers to any income not used for immediate consumption. In economics, savings is defined as income minus consumption. The rate at which people are expected to do this, is called the marginal propensity to save or average propensity to save. The rate of savings is directly related to both the interest rate and investment. It is worth noting that some investment is considered as savings. May I advise that you place your money in banks. Why? Because banks remain the safest legal institutions to save your money. The advantage is that you are entitled to a percentage of interest monthly or annually. You can also access your money at any time you want.

What is Investment?

Investment, according to dictionary definition is "the action or process of investing money for profit or material result." To invest is to allocate money in the expectation of some benefit in the future. You invest with the sole purpose of getting a profitable return, which could be capital gain such as dividends or interest.

Investment generally results in acquiring an asset, also called an investment. If the asset is available at a price worth investing, it is normally expected either to generate income, or to appreciate in value, so that it can be sold at a higher price (or both).

Investors generally expect higher returns from riskier investments. When you "invest," you have a greater chance of losing your money than when you "save."

But when you invest, you also have the opportunity to earn more money than when you save. There is a tradeoff between the higher risk of investing and the potential for greater rewards.

A couple of years ago I advised our young people in Young Disciples International (YDI) to cultivate the culture of saving and investment. Today, this advice is paying off as many of them have assets they never thought they would have in their wildest imagination. Investment is like a seed planted with a hope of having multiple seeds in return or you call it a sacrifice made for a better tomorrow.

Some Few Examples of sectors to invest in:

1. Stock Market

Many of the companies listed on the stock exchange market are successful companies who seek investment from various people in order to be stronger and to have resources to win competition in their various industries. When you acquire a certain number of shares in such a quoted company, you will then become a shareholder. This makes you an automatic "partner" to the owners of such companies.

Advantage of this kind of investment is that, you are not going to be involved in the day to day running or battles of the business world as regards the company you invest in, except of course if you actually own a lion share in the total company's shares.

You also have the advantage of earning 100%, 500% or even 1000% Return on Investment (ROI) just by investing your money in one of the companies listed on the Stock Exchange Market. But there is a caveat here! You can lose your money too. This is not about investing in stock alone, in fact, this is a major phenomena in the business world.

2. Real Estate Market

In most countries of the world real estate business remains an indefatigable investment choice for so many people who really want to become rich and wealthy. Recently I was in Rwandan capital, Kigali for missions; and I discovered that the demand for properties has been on the increase. I also learnt from some Rwandan brethren that many Israeli real estate business gurus have been buying over properties in some strategic locations with the sole purpose of erecting apartment buildings that would be raking in money in no distant future.

It is important that you know that your Return on Investment (ROI) would not come as fast as other sectors of the economy that you invest in. People with investment mind in real estate are keen on buying lands or properties that are cheap knowing that in the next few years such investments will be gold! There is caveat here too! This business can also go bad!

Toyin Ayandare, one of my beloved daughters in the Lord is into real estate in UK. She has the knack for finding cheap and old properties that some people are tired of, then she goes ahead to buy them and renovate them with a view to reselling them at higher rates. What a smart business lady, you would say!

If the Lord is leading you into real estate business, first make sure you read good books on the subject for further knowledge, insights or ideas. The current president of USA, Donald Trump is a genius or guru in real estate business with outstanding books on the subject that will help you. Another American real estate guru, Robert Allen, believes that the number one thing anybody needs, to be a good investor, is business education and investment skills. Do search for good books on real estates in bookstores or online and read them. It will also be an added advantage to attend real estate business seminars.

3. Agriculture and Food business

Investment in agriculture and food business is wise step in the right direction. Wise and prudent farmers will be rich and wealthy. People in food industry that know their onions will be rich and wealthy. The reason is that food is a necessity for human existence and wellbeing. People will always eat! And they will pay for what they eat. You may not have money to buy clothes, but you must look for money to buy food for sustenance and survival. Any investment that brings food to the table is a wise investment!

You can invest in snail, fish or poultry farming. You can invest in food business. Investment in rice farming could yield a good return because rice has become a staple food in Nigeria. Whether we like it or not, oil will not be the hope of our future economy in the nearest future. Agriculture sector will be.

May I end this chapter with a few nuggets I believe will help you save and increase your wealth:

Live within your means

A lot of people try to keep up with the joneses.

You want to look like your friend or neighbor but you don't earn what your friend or neighbor earns.

Be wise! Be disciplined! Be content! Never borrow to finance your life style. It is foolishness to do so!

At least save 10% of your income

Try to save at least 10% of what you earn every month! This is very important because it is only through your savings that you can generate wealth. Remember cash is king.

Embrace knowledge

Be financially literate! I cannot overemphasize this point enough! Acquire knowledge on how to save and invest. The Bible says, "My people are destroyed for lack of knowledge..." (Hosea 4:6)

This is so true in every aspect of our lives including our finances. You cannot aspire to become rich and wealthy and not know how to acquire wealth. Endeavor to educate yourself by reading relevant books! Listen to speakers who are financially literate and learn from them. Above all, develop the habit of always asking questions.

Never leave money idle

Your money should always work for you. Hence the monies you save should never be left idle in a saving account. Never give your money to the banker for free; ensure you get paid for putting your money in the bank. To achieve this, endeavour to put your savings in a fixed deposit account, that way, even when you are sleeping, your money is working for you.

Embrace Guaranteed return

My protégé, Mrs Ifeoma Okoli, who is an investment guru advised that we should never invest all our savings into a venture that does not have a guaranteed return! This is because we could lose all our money if the business venture goes bad. Wisdom demands that you never put all your eggs in one basket. Ensure that part of your savings is in fixed income instruments such as fixed deposits, money market mutual funds or treasury bills.

If you can put into practice the few nuggets shared above, I believe you can truly begin your journey out of poverty.

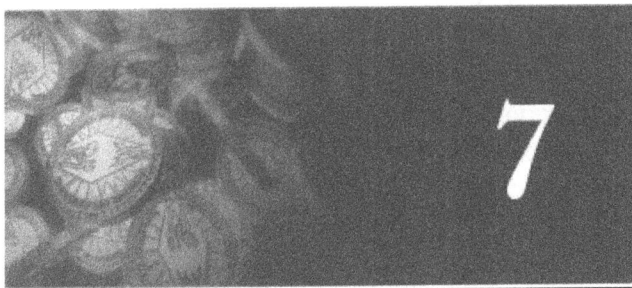

7 CRISIS-PROOFING YOUR BUSINESS AND INVESTMENTS

In these days of economic brouhaha or challenges, can one become rich and wealthy? Can one even maintain sustainable wealth? Can one crisis-proof or bulletproof one's business? Yes of course!

As a business person or an entrepreneur, you must be on guard to bulletproof your business against the ever changing economic weather. For instance, government fiscal and monetary policies are not stable. We have so much government intervention and inconsistency in the running of our economy. And since you cannot influence or alter the government's decisions, you must be ever prepared to swiftly adjust your business to prevent it from being hit by the adverse effect of unfavorable government policies. Bill Gates said, "How fast a company can respond in an emergency is a measure of its corporate reflexes."

Due to the energy crisis bedeviling our country Nigeria, many companies have relocated to neighboring countries, such as Benin Republic and Ghana. It is obvious that some business people hate change, some resist change while others embrace change. Change is constant, so it is either you align your business with the trend and ride to the top or you remain stagnant and eventually fold up. Staying in Nigeria where you don't have guarantee of electricity to power your operations is foolhardiness.

The location of a business is such an important factor that can never be over emphasized. If your business is located in an interior area than your competitor's, you are bound to fail. Factors to consider when choosing a business location are, road network, nearness to high traffic zone, accessibility and patronage level of customers, population, demographics and so on. For example, imagine a business that sells motivational books, located in a brothel. What do you expect? Nothing but outright failure.

5 ways to crisis-proof your Business

1. Keep upgrading your Technological strength

You can crisis proof your business by embracing and upgrading your technological strength as swiftly as possible. Ajaero Tony Martins said, "Your greatest and most powerful business survival strategy is going to be the speed at which you handle the speed of change. That speed of change is trend."

As an entrepreneur, you must be on your toes sniffing the air for available trends and new technologies you can take advantage of. Examples of great industrial trends and technologies are computers, e-shops on the internet, automated accounting, e-payment and so on. Remember, trend is your friend, not your enemy.

2. Keep Strengthening your Management

Do you know why some businesses fail to survive?

The reason is because business owners fail to strengthen their management. A standing rule in the business world is this: "The success or failure rate of any business is directly proportional to the strength and level of professionalism of the management."

From the first day of business, a very strong management is needed to ensure the survival of your business. You might say employing professionals such as attorneys and accountants is very expensive but they will do your business good in the long run. It is a wise step if you can consider bringing in these professionals as partners. By applying this method, you will not pay them salaries while employing their services but they will share in the profit of the business. It is a win-win situation. No matter what tactics you wish to apply, ensure you have a strong management strategy.

When an entrepreneur lacks the necessary skills such as leadership skill, cash flow management, sales, persistence and self belief and so on; such an entrepreneur is bound to fail. An entrepreneur is the head and pilot of the business. Consider an airplane being flown by an inexperienced young pilot? The outcome is disaster waiting to happen.

3. Keep working ahead of your Competitors

Most small business owners are afraid of competition because many profitable ventures have been forced to shut down due to fierce competition. I want to let you know that even if you are the inventor of an idea, that will not stop competitors from coming in. When I started youth ministry in 1996 with my wife, only very few of us were in the trenches of youth work but today many people have come on board doing great things for God. Victor Kiam said, "In business, the competition will bite you if you keep running. If you stand still, they will swallow you." So your best bet is to keep an eye on your competitors, utilize every available innovative idea and make your customers happy by giving them the best products or services.

4. Keep dealing with any saboteur within

You can crisis-proof against the influence of saboteurs within your company. The truth is that saboteurs are real! Employees that corner your customers or clients are your enemies within. Those that pilfer your financial and material resources are saboteurs. Decide to decisively deal with them before they cause any major financial or business havoc. Bad employees can be a chief cause of failure of any business. When you have illegal business transactions and cash siphoning being carried out by employees at the expense of the business, that business is bound to face liquidation.

You must keep a keen eye on the activities of all your employees with respect to the business. It is wise to engage the help of experts. Please check out this profound quote from "The Mafia Manager":

"There will be times when you will have to be abrasive, even brutal to members of your staff.

Don't worry that your people will say bad things about you because of this. They already have. But in general, try to be pleasant and accommodating. Try to please the greatest number who work for you that you can; antagonize the fewest. Blow smoke."

5. Keep Checkmating your Arch-enemy, the devil

You can only checkmate your arch enemy, the devil through the power of God. The devil is a spirit being, as such, your scientific, technological, physical or human strength is useless when it comes to battling with this wicked enemy. You need to depend on God's might, power and wisdom. "Through God we shall do valiantly: for he it is that shall tread down our enemies." (Psalms 60:12)

Are you aware that the devil has been in the business of devouring people, businesses and investments for centuries? He has experience in warfare tactics. He has, with his cohorts, masterminded the failure of many businesses. But your business can be exempt! You can stop or frustrate this devourer from devouring your business and investments via your covenant practice of tithing. God has promised to rebuke the devourer for your sake if you tithe. Do your part and watch Him do His part of the covenant. The Bible says, "Bring ye all the tithes into the storehouse, that there may be meat in mine house, and prove me now herewith, saith the LORD of hosts, if I will not open you the windows of heaven, and pour you out a blessing, that there shall not be room enough to receive it. And I will rebuke the devourer for your sakes, and he shall not destroy the fruits of your ground; neither shall your vine cast her fruit before the time in the field, saith the LORD of hosts." (Malachi 3:10-11)

Do you want to eat the good of the land as far as wealth and riches are concerned? Are you interested in protecting and preserving your business and investment from the devourer? Then embrace a lifestyle of obedience. Do what God says! It pays to obey Him! The Bible says, "If ye be willing and obedient, ye shall eat the good of the land: But if ye refuse and rebel, ye shall be devoured with the sword: for the mouth of the LORD hath spoken it." (Isaiah 1:19-20)

Welcome to your season of great riches and wealth!

OTHER BOOKS BY THE AUTHOR

Building an Effective youth Ministry

Securing your Marital destiny

Get Motivated! Who says you can't make it?

Hebrew Women's Style

How to Obtain Favour from God and Man

Young but Mighty

Essentials of Career Choice

The youth God Uses

Understanding Courtship and Premarital Issues

Questions that Singles Ask - Vol.1

Strategies for Stress free Relationships

Can Boys and Girls also go to Hell?

Child Neglect: Is the Church Guilty?

Teenagers and Relationships

Youth and Friendship

Youth and opportunity

Striving for Excellence

Enjoying God's Mercy

Getting What you Want by Faith

www.ingramcontent.com/pod-product-compliance
Lightning Source LLC
Chambersburg PA
CBHW071925020426
42331CB00010B/2729